FAUX FLOWERS

FAUX FLOWERS

SIMPLE ACCENTS AND ARRANGEMENTS

By Richard Kollath with Ed McCann

Photographs by Roy Gumpel

CHRONICLE BOOKS

SAN FRANCISCO

Library of Congress Cataloging-in-Publication Data available.

ISBN: 0-8118-3374-7

Manufactured in China

Designed by Gretchen Scoble Design

Distributed in Canada by Raincoast Books
9050 Shaughnessy Street
Vancouver, British Columbia V6P 6E5

10 9 8 7 6 5 4 3 2 1

Chronicle Books LLC
85 Second Street
San Francisco, California 94105

www.chroniclebooks.com

This book is in celebration of my parents, John and Ruth Kollath,
who guided and enriched my life.

Contents

Introduction

There's nothing quite like an arrangement of fresh flowers to bring beauty, color, and grace to a room. Or is there?

The truth is, attractive arrangements of faux flowers—whether silk, dried, or preserved—can mimic their fresh counterparts in almost every way, and the advantages are clear: A faux floral arrangement or plant requires no care, is tolerant of fluctuating light and temperature conditions, and lasts indefinitely. These arrangements are also an ideal solution for people with allergies who love having flowers in their homes but not enough to suffer the sniffles and irritated eyes that accompany them.

As the son of florists, I grew up with my dad tending the fields and greenhouses while my mother made arrangements and managed the shop. My mother was a very talented floral designer with a real respect for nature. She wouldn't dye flowers to match someone's dress or shoes, but instead worked to show a client all the complementary and contrasting colors of flowers available in the cooler.

When "artificial" flowers first came into the marketplace, they were plastic and clumsy and awful, and for years my mother refused to stock them. As faux flowers evolved and became more lifelike, she began to have more frequent requests for them, at which point she began experimenting with handmade silk flowers imported from Italy. These arrangements were so convincing she could have placed them in the cooler beside the fresh ones, with no one the wiser. In time, faux flowers became a regular part of our business, and I learned by observation that good design is good design, regardless of the medium.

Having grown up in the fresh flower business, it's somewhat ironic that I should produce a book about faux flowers, but this book isn't my first acquaintance with them. Several years ago, I spent some time in Asia designing silk floral pieces for export to the U.S. market. At the silk flower factories, I looked through countless drawers containing petals of every conceivable shape and color. Before my eyes, these were transformed by nimble fingers into flowers that often closely mirrored nature. Other times, these same petals were recolored for a more dramatic effect, or in response to market demands and decorating trends, sometimes with rather bizarre, unnatural results. Blue and brown roses come to mind.

Why does anybody bring flowers into his or her environment? I think we do so because flowers are one of nature's gifts. They please us with their color, their form, and their scent, and they link us to the world outside our home, most often reflecting the season. Faux flowers can do all but one of these things, which is to provide a fragrance—a fair trade-off for their longevity and ease of care. I enjoy fresh flowers in my home, and with periodic maintenance, a fresh arrangement might look good for as long as a week. A faux arrangement, however, will last until you tire of it. Likewise, a fresh flower would quickly bake and wilt on the dashboard of that parked Volkswagen Beetle, but a silk Gerbera daisy will hold its color and form for many months—or longer.

For many people, ready-made silk arrangements are the only floral element that comes into their home. These purchased arrangements are then parked in one spot and left to grow faded and tired. In fact, there are many ways to use and reuse faux flowers to create a variety of arrangements for many occasions and locations. Like their fresh counterparts, they can be changed or shifted periodically for a fresh effect.

My friend Emma says that when she had her first apartment in New York City, her idea of floral decorating was "to go to the Korean grocer on the corner, buy a bunch of eucalyptus, then stick it in a vase and let it grow dust for four years." While Emma's crisp, dusty eucalyptus might have been appreciated as a sculptural form, I think the key to keeping a faux floral arrangement feeling fresh is to change it every so often—perhaps just seasonally, or when hosting friends. It should brighten and complement your interior landscape rather than disappear into it.

Today, an extraordinary variety of beautiful silk and dried flowers from around the world is widely available in national chain stores as well as through smaller craft shops and florists. Silk and dried flowers are a practical and economical alternative for people too pressed for time to remember to change an arrangement's water, to make fresh cuts on the stems, and to replace them when they droop and fade.

As a designer, I work with a great deal of fresh floral and plant material, but the parameters of certain assignments naturally lend themselves to faux alternatives, particularly in photo studios where live products are exposed to hot lights, and in retail environments where a client hasn't the staff or budget to provide the proper care required to keep fresh flowers looking their best. For many people pressed by the demands of work, family, and maintaining a home, faux is the way to go.

Faux Flowers is a style and how-to book on silk and dried flower projects, providing you with the keys to creating simple, attractive faux floral displays as well as suggestions for ways to use them in your home or in other environments. This book is really about the ease and simplicity of purchasing appealing components to create a sophisticated personal statement, sometimes even incorporating found elements from nature like pinecones, seedpods, acorns, and twigs.

If you purchase a foundation of faux greens that you like, you could simply add or change the blossoms periodically to reflect the season or your mood. It might be convenient to keep a variety of silk stems in a storage box tucked under your bed for this purpose. Consider daffodils, tulips, or peonies for the spring, and hydrangea, bear grass, or roses during the summer. In the fall, you might enjoy some brightly colored zinnias or sunflowers, shifting to some simple branches with berries—or even a bowl of pinecones and seedpods—in the winter.

Most of the arrangements you see in these pages provide instant gratification. With very little skill, effort, or money, they can be completed in just a few steps. My goal in creating this book was to provide you with lots of ideas that you could easily adapt to your own space. I also wanted to include a collection of arrangements whose construction could be understood simply by looking at them, without making you read boring and complicated instructions. Using widely available materials, and employing simple, sometimes surprising techniques, I've translated a variety of ideas into arrangements meant to inspire your creativity. These arrangements are successful because they're uncomplicated, and the simplest arrangements are often the most beautiful, like the richly textured fountain of China millet on page 52, the single pink rose on page 67, and the compact grouping of parrot tulips on page 104.

Even if you have no experience arranging flowers, I think you'll find the process both simple and soothing. A real satisfaction comes from making all the creative decisions involved—from choosing the colors of the flowers and the shape of the container to deciding where you'll display and enjoy your arrangements. In the pages that follow, you'll find basic information on the fundamentals of arranging that will help orient you and get you started. The "Materials" section provides a little background on the range of products available to you and illustrates just how little you really need to begin creating. The section on "Containers" that follows depicts vases and vessels of different shapes, sizes, and materials and explores their different applications. The "Design" section covers some basic principles I think you'll find useful, both in terms of creating arrangements and placing them in your home. "Construction" covers the simple mechanics of putting your arrangements together. Finally, "Arrangements" shows you how to create stunning single-stem arrangements, tall bouquets, compact designs, and plantings.

When you're ready to make your own arrangements, keep in mind that the leap from idea to execution can be a very short one. Whether you live in a city, a suburb, or the country, the materials you need to create a faux arrangement are readily available and fairly inexpensive. You can create something beautiful very quickly that will transform and enliven your home. My hope is that in reading this book, you'll feel inspired and encouraged to experiment. Above all, arranging faux flowers should be fun.

Materials

AN EXPLORATION OF TOOLS AND SUPPLIES

In recent years, remarkable advances have been made in the look and feel of silk flowers. Actually made of polyester and sometimes referred to in the industry as "permanent flowers" and "permanent foliage," their often incredible realism is the result of innovations in molding, heat stamping, and dyeing techniques that result in stems and blossoms that are almost indistinguishable from those produced by nature. I've frequently seen people standing just a few feet away from a faux arrangement move in for a closer look, tentatively touching a leaf or sniffing a flower in disbelief. I recently placed some "permanent plants" in the lobby of a New York City hotel that were so convincing the staff began watering them, not discovering their error until the day the pots began to overflow.

Some silk flowers on the market today have smooth, waterproof stems, coated and sealed with a pliable plastic. Unlike traditional stems, which consist of wire wrapped in green paper tape, you *can* put these plastic stems in water. Some silk flowers are designed specifically for this purpose, and I recently saw hydrangea blossoms meant to float, perhaps with candles, in a shallow bowl. The addition of water takes the floral illusion to a new height, and the interplay of light and water gives an arrangement in a clear container another dimension.

While it can be fun, and in some cases even appropriate, to design with unnaturally hot colors or oversized flowers (I've seen cabbage roses as big as a human head), I prefer to work with faux flowers that mimic nature in every possible way. I tend to shy away from oddly colored flowers—those in the mauve range or the "antique" range, for example— because to me, they're an artificial representation of a flower. What I'm after is something that really fools the eye, and a simple, well-made white or yellow rose contains all the subtlety and poetry of the real thing—minus the scent, of course.

The incredible variety of silk floral products now available provides you—the designer— with a very broad range of choices, broader, in fact, than if you were working with fresh material, because the supply isn't affected by seasonal availability.

Dried or preserved flowers and other natural components also offer a wide scope of design options. I've used dried materials for years to construct wreaths and centerpieces featured in my earlier books. Arrangements of dried flowers have a beautiful, distinctive appearance, but you aren't likely to mistake them for fresh. In the projects featured in these pages, I've focused predominantly on arrangements of silk flowers, experimenting with occasional additions of dried ingredients to heighten their realism.

Augmenting a silk arrangement with natural dried materials can provide a refreshing counterpoint. Even at a 90 percent silk to 10 percent dry ratio, the combination of these materials presents an opportunity to juxtapose differing textures in a way that really fools the eye. If, for example, an arrangement of silk flowers seems a bit too perfect (and therefore unnatural), the addition of some dried yarrow, millet, or wheat can make your arrangement really stunning. Similarly, a manufactured "evergreen" holiday garland appears much more lush and natural when you attach some pinecones with florist wire, or when a small amount of seeded eucalyptus or manzanita is added. The visual suggestion can be quite powerful: Last year, a guest at the Ahwahnee Hotel in Yosemite National Park paused to watch while a crew and I rigged a scentless artificial Christmas garland over a large fireplace mantle. She closed her eyes, inhaled deeply, and said, "Oh, I just love the smell of fresh greens!"

It's easy to dry your own fresh material using silica gel, but the marketplace is filled with a large variety of inexpensive dried and preserved flowers, grasses, and pods. Some of my favorites are lavender, globe thistle, globe amaranth, cock's comb, galax leaf, phalaris, holly, and juniper. Humble sticks and twigs make interesting design contributions, too, and natural raffia can be used to tie a silk orchid stem to a stake or to wrap a container with leaves.

I particularly like preserved oak leaves, which are available in their entire color range, from pale green to gold and fiery red. Their color and pliability are remarkably close to that of fresh oak leaves, and they work especially well in autumn arrangements.

Many elements can be picked or purchased fresh, then simply arranged in a container—without water—and allowed to dry on their own. Pussy willow, hydrangea, eucalyptus, yarrow, strawflower, silver dollar, and statice are some good examples. Twigs, branches, and pods can also be combined to create a refined, unique arrangement. Combining artificial and natural material creates textural juxtapositions that also fool the eye.

Don't miss an opportunity to collect beautiful things from nature when you can. Friends joke that I must have been a hunter-gatherer in a former life, because when I'm walking or hiking through the mountains near my Hudson River Valley home, I tend to fill my pockets with interesting pinecones or seedpods. A trip to the beach generally yields some shells and sea glass. Many of these things find their way into a photograph and end up in an ever-changing still life composition of natural elements in a large wooden tray in my studio.

THE ONLY TOOLS REQUIRED TO MAKE THE ARRANGEMENTS YOU SEE IN THESE photographs are a pair of scissors to trim leaves and a good-quality pair of wire cutters. Thick flower stems often contain heavy gauge wires, or several wires bound together, which can be difficult to cut through. Your hands will quickly become fatigued if you're struggling to cut these stems with light-duty wire cutters, so I suggest you purchase—or borrow—a good pair of lineman's cutters. Silk and dried floral foam, sometimes sold under the trade name "Sahara," is used to anchor stems in opaque containers, though you might prefer to use florist "frogs," pebbles, stones, or even pinecones. I'll talk more about anchoring in the section on construction.

This bears mentioning again: When you decide to shop for faux flowers, take the vase or other container you'll be using with you to gauge accurately the length and number of stems you'll need to fill it. And when you're thinking about where to place your new arrangement, try to keep it out of direct sunlight. As with any textile, natural or synthetic, it will become faded with constant exposure to ultraviolet light.

Very few tools or supplies are necessary to create a faux floral arrangement. Wire cutters, a kitchen knife, and floral foam are just about all you'll need to create any of the arrangements shown in this book. Stems in transparent containers can be arranged without any anchoring medium, but they allow for options such as pebbles or, when appropriate, the addition of water. A small block of floral foam can be used to anchor stems in opaque containers. ✿

A metal or glass frog placed in a container can be used as an alternative to floral foam to hold and direct the stems. These frogs are available where floral supplies are sold, and you'll also find them frequently in tag sales and antique shops. ✿

Just purchased at the market, this woven strap bag of silk daisies is filled with potential. Arranged singly, in a group, or combined in an arrangement with other flowers, daisies add a fresh look to any environment. When shopping for faux flowers, check several sources, since quality varies widely. ✿

The only care a faux floral arrangement requires is an occasional dusting. You can gently shake the dust off the stems outdoors, or you can use a blow-dryer. Silk flowers can be rinsed with tepid water, providing the stems are sealed plastic, not wrapped in green paper. Spread the flowers out on a towel to air dry, then reassemble your arrangement. Try to minimize handling the blossoms themselves, as their edges may begin to ravel. Errant threads can be trimmed with a pair of sharp scissors. ✿

Containers

STYLES, TYPES, AND SIZES

Whether you begin with a container or with a bunch of flowers, the container you choose for an arrangement will, in some ways, dictate the scale of the flowers you'll use in it as well as their quantity and the length of their stems. There are probably as many containers available to you as there are flowers to put in them, in an almost limitless variety of shapes and sizes. The "vase" you choose might actually be a bottle, pitcher, box, eggcup, bucket, flowerpot, wicker basket, or fishbowl.

Let's think in terms of two broad categories of containers—transparent and opaque. You'll see several examples of each type of container in the following photographs. An opaque container hides the "works"—the frog, floral foam, or other means of support you'll use to hold your stems in place. A transparent container, in contrast, allows you to see the flower stems, making them part of the arrangement. It can be fun to add water to an arrangement in a clear container or an attractive anchoring medium, such as pebbles or sea glass. Remember, you should only use water in arrangements of sealed plastic stems, not of paper-wrapped wire stems, which will quickly begin to degrade and rust.

A clear glass cylinder is a favorite choice of mine. It's a classic shape that's available in many sizes, from short and squat to tall and slender. It doesn't call attention to itself but directs your focus to the material contained within it. I've sometimes filled glass cylinders with nuts, limes, crab apples, pinecones, and many other things—with or without flowers. Colored glass vessels are also quite interesting and can provide you with an opportunity to cue the colors of the flowers you choose for them, either contrasting or complementary.

Opaque containers can be metal, ceramic, wood, or any number of other materials. And since your silk, dried, or preserved stems aren't relying on a supply of water, you can really push the envelope with an unusual vessel like a large seashell, which would be impractical for a fresh arrangement.

Use care to choose a vase that isn't too large for the quantity of stems you'll be working with, or your arrangement will look skimpy. The right size container will result in an arrangement that appears lush and abundant. If you place the same flowers in different containers, you'll notice the varied effects created by different combinations: The same iris that looks so elegant in a silver trumpet becomes informal, even whimsical, in a tiny ceramic garden boot. The flowers will relate in unique ways to the container you select, and they will also interact with the environment you choose for them, based on lighting and the other objects and textures in the room. Experiment with containers of different proportions and characteristics to determine what pleases you.

Home accessory stores are good design sources for flower containers, but don't forget to look around your own home—or the homes of friends and family—for interesting vases that might just be collecting dust or loose change. Flea markets, antique shops, and tag sales often yield eclectic containers for very little money, but one of the best resources might be grandma's attic or your brother's basement, where a disused or forgotten vessel might be waiting to be brought back into the light. Found objects lend a special charm to an environment. A reclaimed container, like your grandfather's trophy or your mother's milk glass trumpet vase, contributes to your personal style and allows you to enjoy not only your floral arrangement but also a sense of your history, too.

Silk and dried flowers can be used separately or in combination to create a variety of arrangements for your coffee table, bedside table, dining table, desk, windowsill, sink, or any other surface. When purchasing flowers, bring the container you plan to use to the store with you. This will help you select the right sizes and quantities of materials.

Selecting a container for your faux floral arrangement presents almost as many choices as you have for the flowers you'll put inside them. This collection of clear, pale, and opaque glass containers shows a range of possibilities, including a contemporary cube, a pressed-glass pitcher, and a milk glass fan, discovered at a tag sale for a dollar. A variety of factors will affect the container you choose and largely determine the effect you'll create with your arrangement: Will the stems be visible? How will the width of the opening affect their placement? Where will the arrangement be displayed? Experiment with different shapes, and you'll quickly find your favorites. ✿

Any one of these brilliantly colored glass vases would create a strong impression in your environment and would filter light in a dramatic way—as if through a jewel or a stained-glass window. Consider the interesting effect that pairing a few simple greens or white flowers would create with one of these amethyst, cobalt, or peridot vases. You might also choose flowers in the vase's complementary color—yellow blossoms in blue glass, for example. No matter what you put in containers like these, their color greatly affects your overall design. ✿

These opaque ceramic containers illustrate a variety of shapes, including an hourglass, a flowerpot, and a bottle. You could also use a tea cup, compote, or any appealing form—found or purchased—that will hold a block of floral foam in which to anchor your flower stems. ✿

Metal containers offer great versatility, as shown by this grouping of aluminum, tin, iron, copper, and brass. Floral foam wedged inside these vessels creates a secure foundation for virtually any type of faux arrangement, and a block of foam in a wire basket could be concealed with a layer of sheet moss or Spanish moss. Great new metal containers are widely available in design and home decorating stores, and because they aren't fragile like glass or ceramic vases, interesting old vessels frequently turn up in flea markets or attics. Bringing these durable containers with the silent patina of their history into your home—like the boating trophy that belonged to my friend's grandfather, seen on page 35—allows you to enjoy a sense of that history, even if it's not your own. ✿

Low containers like this group of wooden bowls, shallow baskets—even a seashell—are perfect for displaying compact faux floral arrangements. They're also ideal repositories for collections of pods, cones, stones, or any other found or purchased elements that appeal to you. Filled with fruit, coconuts, or autumn leaves, they'd constitute a decorative arrangement all by themselves but can also be dressed up by augmenting them with a few short stems of silk, dried, or preserved flowers. ✿

This is an example of another grouping of elements that, while not containing any actual flowers, represent

other parts of a living plant. A shallow basket filled with pinecones, pears, and both coleus and coral saxifraga

leaves is a subtle texture study composed of muted colors. You can create many variations on this idea—in

a bowl, box, or basket. Use apples, oranges, nuts, or other components, changing the greens to reflect the

season. You'll be creating a still life that calls to mind the beauty of growing, living things. ✿

Here's a sweet and simple arrangement: A diminutive vase, shaped like a pair of gardener's boots, contains silk Dutch iris and a few fern stems—a mix of elements you might come up with if you'd picked things from your own garden. ✿

Found objects often seem to carry their stories with them. When poking through an attic or perusing tables at a flea market, be on the lookout for funky or unusual containers that can add a sense of history to an arrangement.

Unusual found objects often make interesting containers for flower arranging. A friend recently rediscovered her grandfather's old boating trophy and found it to be just the right proportion for a loose arrangement of snapdragons, which she's displayed in her home office. In addition to enjoying the lush appearance of these tall, colorful stems, she appreciates that the arrangement represents a sentimental connection to a family member and that it resonates with personal history. A bit of fresh grapevine in a florist's water pick provides a softening counterpoint to the tall stems—a quick and easy addition for a special occasion. ✿

Let's say you have an idea for an arrangement for your side table. When you're shopping in the aisle with all those buckets of faux flowers, gather some stems in your hand, thinking, "I'd like to use this with this . . . and this." Looking at the bunch of flowers you're now holding gives you a good sense of the volume of foliage and flowers you'd be working with. But what you're holding is all bunched up, and all the stems are straight. Imagine how much fuller and softer these things will appear once you've opened their leaves and maneuvered the blossoms into a more lifelike appearance.

Design

BASIC PRINCIPLES FOR CREATING AND USING FAUX FLORAL ARRANGEMENTS

Many of you reading this book will simply want to know why an arrangement "works" and how you can produce your own arrangements successfully. I don't want to dictate a list of rules, because I think they're a real constraint to creativity. There are some basic guidelines, however, that when followed contribute to an arrangement's success, regardless of whether you're working with faux or fresh flowers: try to select an appropriate container for your flowers; make shifts in scale, color, and texture; and create balance and counterbalance. These are the same principles that contribute to an attractive meal, a comfortably decorated room, or a well-designed landscape. Throughout this book, I point out examples of these principles, showing you how to adapt and incorporate them into your own designs.

Floral design, like fashion, goes through cycles. In the world of professional flower arranging, there have been many popular trends that appear somewhat dated today, like the flowing S-shaped arrangements called "Hogarth Curves." Some of the standard florist shop offerings we've grown so used to seeing—fan-shaped pom-poms with leatherleaf fern, red roses in baby's breath—have a homogenized, by-the-numbers quality and do little to inspire. Illustrated step-by-step for the industry in trade manuals, these arrangements are designed to adhere to a somewhat rigid standard, using floral materials available year-round at low cost from the suppliers. This is why you'll find virtually the same types of arrangements in Kansas City or Quebec. Certainly many talented florists regularly break free from these design constrictions, but the market has come to expect these offerings of the lowest common denominator, and only a small percentage of customers are willing to pay a premium for creativity.

What we're seeing a lot of today in magazines and high-end florist shops is a style of arranging that involves cutting a dense bundle of stems to a uniform length and jamming them into a clear vase with their stems exposed. These costly modernist arrangements, fast becoming a cliché, appear deceptively simple, when in fact they're not. But there is a dominant design movement that more or less dictates "This is how we do it," and brides-to-be all over the country are clipping the same pictures from magazines to show to their florists. Keep in mind that just as there is no one way to assemble a salad, there is also no single correct method of constructing a floral arrangement.

I grew up during a time when the prevailing style of flower arranging was somewhat stiff and predictable, but what I learned by watching my parents working in their flower shop was to look to nature for inspiration. Despite all the formulas and industry recipes for flower arrangements, I continue to feel that an arrangement, whether fresh or faux, speaks best when it contains an element of abstraction or surprise. Tuck some things into a bridal bouquet that only the bride will see, putting blossoms behind greenery where they can be discovered upon closer inspection. Or do something as simple as putting a single stem in a vase, without stripping its leaves—things that mirror nature with grace and spirit, complementing the individual flower.

As you begin experimenting with your own arrangements, remember that you're not after symmetry or precision or perfection—goals that are likely to frustrate you in your attempts and cause you to become discouraged. Remember that it's those shifts in scale, color, texture, and balance I spoke about earlier that will make your arrangements unique and sophisticated, elevating them in their tastefulness above some of the more common and predictable "premade" arrangements you'll find in a store.

At its simplest, floral arranging is about the relationship between a container and a flower. In arrangements with multiple stems, it's also about the flowers' relationships to one another. Finally, it's about placement. Where will you put your arrangement? You'll make particular design decisions based on whether it's to be in the center of a dining table, next to a lamp, or on a surface all by itself, which allows for a grander, stronger presence.

The following pages reflect a variety of arrangement styles, and though some may appear to be elaborate, they're actually all fairly simple to execute. They incorporate lovely flowers with beautiful, but perhaps unrelated, greens as well as some other secondary elements. While you can certainly reproduce the arrangements you see in these photographs stem for stem, I encourage you to follow your own instincts and begin to experiment. There's great satisfaction in learning to trust your own eye, your own hand. Take your cues from nature, the best designer of all. You'll create something beautiful and lasting for your environment, and you'll do it with pleasure and ease.

Before you start assembling your faux floral arrangement—or even purchasing the components to make it—consider the effect you want to create. Are you looking for a cheerful burst of color on an end table? Perhaps you'd like something tall and loose for your entrance, or a low, compact arrangement for the kitchen or dining room. A common mistake is to place a tall arrangement on a dining table, which interferes with your dinner companions' ability to see one another. While the mechanics of building a faux arrangement are quite simple, it's useful to have a mental picture of what sort of arrangement you're trying to achieve, as well as of where you intend to display it, before you begin.

As you're assembling your arrangement, think about balance and counterbalance, being mindful of the contrasting forms, colors, and textures developing before you. Look at the position of the individual flowers; they shouldn't all face forward—you should see sides and backs as well, just as you would in a garden. Get your inspiration by looking at nature—the surprises, imperfections, and sense of depth that occur without any help from a human hand. Notice the way a blossom hides itself among the others. Proceed with a light hand. The more you work with flowers, whether faux or fresh, the more confident you'll become in your arranging abilities.

When making a fresh floral arrangement, only the stems should be below the waterline, not the leaves. Stems draw water and feed the blossoms, while leaves quickly decompose, turning the water murky. For your faux arrangement to have an authentic appearance, you should strip these lower leaves as well.

This cheerful grouping of hot-colored Gerbera daisies in clear glass is juxtaposed against the abstract rose lithograph above the mantle. Just seven stems highlighted against the backdrop of a white wall create a dramatic—and inexpensive—design statement. The short stems in tumblers and the candlestick on the right side of the mantle act as a visual counterweight to the arrangement on the left. Sealed plastic stems allow the daisies to be placed in a few inches of water. ✿

Tall white agapanthus stems make a dramatic architectural statement. Heighten their realistic appearance by placing them in a tall crystal cylinder filled with water. As long as the stems are sealed, as these are, they can rest in water without rusting or deteriorating. ✿

Enjoyed as a still life on a side table, coffee table, or dining table, something as simple as a bowl, basket, or platter of fruit—real or faux—brings a natural beauty into your environment. ✿

Seasonal changes make a room feel fresh and reflect your personal spirit in decorating a home. The restrained statement of autumn seen here comprises five elements that combine silk and dried natural materials—a wreath, a large pinecone, gourds, and two faux arrangements. The focal point and anchor of the composition is an oak leaf wreath above the mantle, purchased fresh and green a few years ago. In its first season, the leaves dried and curled naturally, resulting in a very different but still beautiful form. The large sugar pinecone, collected on a hiking trip in northern California, echoes the color and texture of the wreath, and the gourds filling the cement garden urn were purchased green off the vine from a farm stand in New York's Hudson River Valley. All these things are inexpensive and can be used for years in many different ways.

The faux arrangement on the mantle is made of three stems of sweet wood leaning to the left and three delicate sprays of deeply colored pokeberry on the right. There's a real division in this arrangement and a balance of two differently weighted elements. What makes it work is the contrast between the gestures of the sweet wood stems and the visual counterweight of the pokeberry, hanging down from the mouth of the container. The compact arrangement of black-eyed Susans next to the wingback chair makes its own contribution of warm and muted color and adds a lively texture as well. ✿

The simplicity of a single small gourd placed in a yellowware bowl lends a meditative feel to this tranquil little tablescape. An interesting rock, seashell, or any other find from a walk or shopping expedition could just as easily have created this subtle design gesture. ✿

A handful of individual hydrangea florets, which are easily removed from the head, surround a pillar candle on a square silver metal tray. This very simple addition makes for a special presentation. Variations on this idea could include the use of nuts, polished stones, pinecones, sea glass, or any other small objects that would contribute an interesting texture or color. ✿

A single dried maple leaf on a terra-cotta plate is framed in a square woven tray and seems almost suitable for hanging. The interplay between circle and square and the completely muted colors make for an interesting texture study. This representation of a tree is as reduced and refined as a line of poetry. Note how the leaf stem follows the diagonal line of the tray's corners. ✿

A scattering of found elements displayed on a porcelain plate includes acorns, river rocks, and eucalyptus seedpods. Their presence serves as a reminder of the places I gathered these things. The collection will likely be added to over time, growing to include feathers, sea glass, pinecones, and whatever other interesting objects appear in my path. These are things you could add to a potpourri or use to anchor faux floral stems in a transparent container, making them—and your own explorations—part of the arrangement as well. ✿

A primitive, elongated block of wood with a series of drilled, wide holes could inspire many uses for a centerpiece on a long table. Here, the wood's texture and a mixture of short pillar candles and red silk hibiscus blossoms combine to create an arrangement with an exotic feel. Because the blossoms are lower than the candles, there's little risk of fire. You should never leave a burning candle unattended, however, or in a place where a child could reach it. ✿

Construction

FOUNDATIONS AND ASSEMBLY TECHNIQUES

The majority of the arrangements featured in these pages were constructed in one of two ways: either by placing stems directly into a container or by inserting stems into floral foam secured at the base of the container. You could also use a glass or metal frog—a device that's placed at the bottom of a vase to hold and help direct the stems—for this same purpose.

Placing the stems in a few inches of a decorative anchoring medium like pebbles will help keep them in place, too. If you were having a party or hosting a holiday get-together and wanted to do something special, you could arrange some stems in a cylinder filled with lemons, limes, small apples, or pears—things that would stay fresh for a week and that would lend a festive feeling to the arrangement and to the room.

Whether a faux floral stem has a single flower or a cluster of leaves and blossoms, the stem is usually straight as a rod. One way in which a silk arrangement differs from a fresh one is that fresh stems tend to have variations. Some fresh stems are thick and hollow, some flat and twisted, and some are quite delicate, causing them to bend gracefully under the weight of their blossoms. I choose these irregular stems in the fresh flower market because they lend an arrangement a certain spirit that I respond to. They exhibit a natural grace precisely because

An inexpensive urn lends a classical elegance to this simple, dramatic arrangement of natural China millet. Thinking about the way grasses grow in fields, I placed a combination of natural and dyed stems in a block of floral foam for an effect that mimics a flowing fountain. The tan and pale green are close in value, adding visual interest, and the subtle contrast allows the focus to remain on the arrangement's rich textures. ✿

they aren't perfectly uniform. This characteristic helps create unexpected relationships between elements that more closely mimic what you'll see in nature.

When you're working with permanent flowers, you can gently articulate some of the stems to duplicate the form or habits of natural ones. This doesn't mean you have to bend every stem, but you can soften some of them by taking them individually in both hands and working them to create smooth, subtle curves and bends.

The forms of the flowers and foliage you're working with will help you determine how to construct your arrangement. Unlike their fresh counterparts, whose delicate stems may require special support techniques, the wire stems of faux flowers make it easy to build a solid foundation, and the leaves on some stems are rigid enough to hold the stem right where you've placed it. Remember, too, that your arrangement will appear stiff and unnatural if all the stems are the same length. Use your wire cutters to vary the lengths of the stems, creating a textural rhythm in your arrangement.

If you're designing an arrangement for a clear container in which the stems will be exposed, begin by placing each stem individually, perhaps first establishing a base of greens followed by your flowers. Since the stems will become an integral part of this arrangement, remove any leaves that would appear below the upper third of the container (in a fresh arrangement, only the stems are underwater, never the leaves, which would quickly decay and turn the water murky). Alternate sides, crossing the stems, and they will soon begin to hold and support one another.

The placement of your first few stems will help determine the overall shape of the arrangement. Stand back from time to time and assess where the arrangement is going. Does it have a front and a back? Will it be seen from all sides? While you're working, strive to create a sense of balance and counterbalance, equalizing the visual weight of your ingredients.

If I'm cutting stems to make a compact arrangement, I find that it's far simpler to put a block of floral foam in the container, then poke the stems individually into place. To construct an arrangement with floral foam, begin by using a knife to cut a block of foam slightly larger than the container. As you push the foam downward into your vase, it will compress slightly to form a snug fit in the bottom.

The process of constructing an arrangement in floral foam is a little slower and more deliberate than the exposed-stem method described earlier, in which you can easily remove and reposition stems to your liking. In this case, begin by holding a stem in front of the container and take a visual measurement for the desired height. Once you've cut the stem, place it in front of the container again to double-check and, if necessary, cut it again before placing it in the foam. The reason you do this is that floral foam will hold the stem firmly the first time you insert it. If you remove the stem to place it into the foam a second time, you will have created a hole or a void in the foam. While the foam is somewhat forgiving, keep in mind that the more holes you create, the more you compromise the foam's ability to keep stems where you want them. If the stems aren't securely anchored, they could become wobbly, or even topple out of your container.

One advantage in constructing arrangements with stems of wire and fabric is the ability to twist or bend foliage to help hold stems in place. In most of the examples you see here, the arranging style is very natural, with the same textural shifts and sense of movement you'd expect to find in a well-designed fresh arrangement.

With faux flowers, we can enjoy almost any flower we want at any time. It's a bit incongruous, however, to display very seasonal flowers like crocus or holly at the wrong time of year.

Ideal for Easter, this charming arrangement of faux grass, pansies, and eggs in a shallow, nest-shaped basket would add a beautiful and whimsical accent to the breakfast table on any spring morning.

Constructing this nest only required me to place a section of grass in the basket, followed, in order, by the eggs and the pansies. This arrangement is so simple that it could quickly and easily be reproduced in multiples for a party or special event. For a simple variation, you might eliminate the eggs and use more pansies, or you might consider using different flowers, perhaps inspired by those you've seen while walking through unmown grass. Diminutive violets, wildflowers, or tiny black-eyed Susans, for example, would appropriately complement the scale of the grass while also changing the arrangement's color temperature, the latter even suggesting a shift from spring to early summer.

Allow yourself the freedom to experiment. Just think for a moment about how dramatically the entire composition would shift if I'd used one more or one less pansy or egg. While just a few humble components are involved here, this is a good illustration of how scale, proportion, and balance combine to create a successful arrangement. ✿

What appears to be an unusual evergreen is actually a form of protea called silver cone, purchased fresh and arranged simply in a flared glass vase. Like eucalyptus, German statice, and many forms of conifer greens, they will hold their form and color as they dry. A handful of sequoia cones allows air to circulate around the stems and adds an interesting texture to an arrangement that could be used as a seasonal or holiday accent. ✿

The colors and textures of the spicy-citrus potpourri in this square glass vase are very pleasing to the eye and make an interesting counterpoint to a loose arrangement of faux cattails. The potpourri also adds a pleasing scent, missing from permanent arrangements, without being cloying or overpowering. ✿

A wreath is a welcoming addition to an entrance door or to any room in your home. Placed on a horizontal surface instead of a vertical one, a wreath becomes an instant centerpiece. Here, a dried bay leaf wreath from the kitchen rings a lantern with a white pillar candle, creating a festive look for the holidays that's also appropriate at any time of year. For a variation, you could use the pillar candle alone or a few tapers in place of the lantern. On a dining table, you might place a bowl of fruit in the center of a wreath, perhaps even scattering some votive candles around the perimeter for a romantic effect.

Premade wreaths are readily available through a variety of sources but can be easily constructed by inserting silk, fresh, or dried stems directly into a wreath form made of straw or grapevine, securing them if necessary with a dab of hot glue. Wreaths can also be made, as this one was, by binding elements onto a sturdy wire ring with waxed cord, monofilament, or thin wire. Standing at a counter-height work surface, begin by tying one end of the cord to the wreath form, then hold a handful of stems against the form and bind them in place by wrapping the cord around both the stems and form. Maintain a uniform tension on the cord while wrapping and binding, positioning each successive bunch of greens so that the bound stems of the last bunch are concealed, continuing until the wreath form is fully concealed.

The construction process is virtually the same whether you use bay leaves, autumn foliage, or even sprigs of evergreens. ✿

A tall vase of white hydrangea and viburnum—also called Snowball bush—is the focal point of a transparent glass tablescape in a light-filled room. Leaves were stripped from the lower stems, and only six or eight stems were required to create the cloudlike feeling of this arrangement. The dark green leaves that remain form an anchoring collar that secures the stems and flowers in place. Tonal variations between flowers in this mono- chromatic grouping add a sense of depth, as if the cloud is darker at its center, and other glass vessels, containing a candle and a goldfish, create a composition that feels practically weightless. The slight visual distortion created by the horizontal ripple design of the vase suggests the presence of water. ❀

A child will often reach for the brightest crayon, but as the eye becomes more sophisticated, we begin to make design choices based on textures and other subtleties. When you're designing in an all-white or other monochromatic palette, the focus is on textural relationships and contrasts in height and form.

Arrangements

SINGLE-STEM

One little flower can make a big difference. A room that previously had no flowers in it can seem dramatically changed by the addition of a single blossom. The eye naturally travels to it, taking in its color, gesture, and form as well as its relationship to the objects surrounding it.

Single-stem arrangements are design studies in the clarity of just two components—blossom and vase. At first glance, these arrangements appear very simple, perhaps like a clear voice singing one note. Other notes are added, however, as you begin to examine and consider the proportional relationship between blossom and container, the angle of the stem, the gesture of the petals and leaves.

Choose any flower that pleases you, or begin by selecting a vase, then match a flower to it. Even more so than with multiple-stem arrangements, the container you select is a key design consideration. It doesn't just support the stem; it visually anchors it to a surface, acting as a counterweight to the blossom. This presents an opportunity to draw attention to a special or unusual vase. The container you choose carries a large proportion of the visual weight and can become the focus.

Successful single-stem arrangements simply require a sensitivity about weight, proportion, and balance. Their construction is as easy as cutting the stem to a pleasing length, perhaps stripping lower leaves, and placing it in its container.

Some of this may seem a bit esoteric, but as you begin to appreciate the sculptural simplicity of a single stem in a container, you'll become more familiar with the principles employed in creating other types of arrangements.

Single-flower arrangements are studies in the purity of form, and this single yellow rose in a hand-blown glass container has a subtle yet commanding presence. The proportional relationship between the blossom and container creates a pleasing balance, and the small opening in the vase allows the stem to remain vertical. The bottom leaves on the stem were stripped; those that remain add contrast and grace. Without them, the rose would appear forlorn. ✿

This fully blown single pink rose blossom rests against the side of a textured amethyst glass cylinder. While the arrangement appears very simple, there's a lot going on here. I chose to display the rose this way because the blossom is a spectacular specimen all by itself. Placing it within a large-mouthed cylinder lends the arrangement a sense of abstraction and simplicity and gives roughly equal visual weight to both elements. The strong diagonal line of the stem and the three leaves inside the cylinder create visual tension. Resting the neck of the rose against the rim, rather than have it poking out above, connects the two elements and brings the subtle textured detail of the vase into focus. ✿

There are some obvious places to use faux floral arrangements—a dining table, end table, coffee table, or desk—but you can use them to brighten and soften other areas of your home as well. Here, a collection of small glass bottles on a kitchen windowsill is pressed into service by five red anemones. This asymmetrical grouping of individual arrangements forms a miniature landscape that can be changed on a whim or with the seasons. Gently articulated petals and varied stem lengths create a pleasing balance, and using water in the bottles creates the illusion that these flowers have just been picked from the garden. ✿

The Asian simplicity of this table centerpiece invites close inspection. A hand-turned wooden bowl displays assorted exotic seedpods I've collected during my travels, juxtaposed with the fresh appearance of a single pink rose blossom cut from its stem. A clean, direct design statement, this still life is really about collecting things you think are beautiful and displaying them together on a bowl or tray, adding or subtracting elements as you wish. The round woven tray underneath echoes the bowl's shape, adding another natural texture to the assemblage. ✿

After countless hours providing light to an earlier generation, these graceful pressed-glass oil lamps—discovered at a yard sale—haven't lost their ability to brighten a room. Without their wicks and fuel supply, their beautiful footed forms make perfect flower containers, for either fresh or faux stems. Here, "cuttings" of permanent white lilac are displayed down the center of a long dining table, creating an inspired landscape-style centerpiece with a decidedly spring feeling. ✿

Faux orchids are among the most convincing silks you'll find, and as an indoor plant, they're appropriate year-round. The color of this yellow tiger orchid pops against the deep painted wall it's displayed against. It took just a few moments to transform this faux orchid plant from a stiff and unnatural state to a graceful, almost exotic statement that beautifully mimics nature. I began by wedging a block of floral foam into a square container with a crackled finish that contributed its own subtle texture.

I secured the plant's wire stem by pushing it downward into the foam base, after which I manipulated the leaves and blossoms into a natural-looking configuration. A thin piece of bamboo was then pushed down into the foam next to the stem and bound to the stem with a length of raffia, ostensibly to support the stem and hold it vertical against the opposing force created by the weight of the branching flowers. I concealed the floral foam with a few scored, freeze-dried limes, purchased from a craft shop. The addition of the bamboo, raffia, and limes—all dry, natural elements—enhances the overall visual presentation of this single stem planting. ✿

TALL BOUQUETS

LIKE SOMEONE STANDING WITH THEIR ARMS OUTSTRETCHED OR OVERHEAD, tall bouquets have a commanding presence. You can choose to mix many different materials or concentrate on arranging a group of one type of flower.

Tall arrangements work well in larger spaces and are best displayed where their height won't interfere with the things surrounding them and where they won't get snagged or toppled by passersby. Generally speaking, you'll want to choose a tall container to support longer stems, and certainly one with enough stability to keep your arrangement from tipping. If top-heavy blossoms are used in a lightweight container, it may be necessary to weight the container with some sand or a few stones.

The construction techniques used for tall arrangements are as direct as any other in this book. Stems visible through their container can be freely arranged or anchored in pebbles or another decorative medium. Stems in an opaque ceramic or metal container can be securely anchored in a block of floral foam.

Tall bouquets can be as traditional as a group of gladiolas in glass, or as abstract as a few bare branches in a bucket. Some flower forms—such as those of the amaryllis or delphinium—more naturally lend themselves to arrangements with height. Whatever materials you choose, tall arrangements allow for a bit of drama and showing off.

Eastern light shining through a handful of blue delphiniums makes a spectacular morning display. Contrasted against a complementary yellow wall, the delphiniums, along with the blue and white Chinese vase that contain them, have a very strong presence in this kitchen. Nearby on the windowsill, a few humble black-eyed Susans in a slender silver trumpet vase appear freshly picked and reflect the kitchen's wall color.

The juxtaposition of these two arrangements in the same space illustrates the qualities they share more than the differences in color and scale that set them apart: A few flowers, simply arranged, is all that it takes to bring beauty and a sense of life to a room. ✿

This loose and unforced grouping of pink and purple cosmos was simple to create. The finished arrangement has a graceful, airy appearance, owing in part to its wide-mouthed container, which allows the stems to "relax." Cosmos are a beautiful summer flower, and their fine, dill-like foliage creates volume and visual interest, giving the arrangement its shape and form without the necessity of additional greens. This arrangement was created by pushing a block of floral foam into a container—in this case a vintage sap bucket—then inserting individual stems into the foam. Once the stems were secured, I maneuvered the heads in a way that made them appear more natural. It's interesting to note that each stem has three flower heads, providing the look of a very full arrangement for the cost of about seven stems. This kind of arrangement would make a beautiful rustic centerpiece, but it would also work in a small space, because it doesn't dominate with any real visual weight. ✿

> *Turning and manipulating some of the leaves and flower heads immediately changes an arrangement's visual configuration, allowing it to appear more natural and expansive and contributing to a very graceful, airy appearance. Stems and petals that are perfectly, uniformly smoothed, opened, and otherwise tweaked look unnatural. When tweaking stems and leaves, try to mimic nature's imperfections.*

Stalks of white amaryllis in a tapered square glass vase make a simple yet sophisticated statement for the holidays. White Christmas balls anchoring the flower stems are an unexpected but attractive addition. They could easily have been red, green, or any other color, giving an entirely different feel to an otherwise monochromatic arrangement. The concrete garden urn filled with dried lavender adds a punch of color and subtle fragrance to the room. ✿

Just four stems of green parrot tulips are all it takes to create an elegant arrangement in this old tin container. The incredible realism is achieved though gentle manipulation of the stems, leaves, and petals, all of which are pretty stiff and uniform when first purchased. You can bring them to life by gently bowing the stems and opening the petals. Open some more than others, to create the appearance that the flowers have been picked at different times. The funky painted vase is a mass-produced commercial vessel whose patina of age makes it look one of a kind. ✿

When purchasing an assortment of flowers for an arrange-
ment, buy like stems in odd groups of three or more. There's
something about odd numbers of flowers that seems to keep
the eye moving around an arrangement and that creates a
more pleasing appearance.

With their fuzzy leaves and stems, these sunflowers are some of the most convincing fakes I've seen, made even more so by placing them in a few inches of water. Two inexpensive amber hurricane lamps establish a compositional symmetry that's knocked a bit off balance by their contents: a tall pillar candle in one lamp, and the grouping of sunflowers in the other. ✿

An exuberant, fan-shaped display of yellow gladiolas in an amethyst glass vase contrasts dramatically with a classic Eero Saarinen table and chairs in an all-white room. A delicate faux olive branch, complete with black olives, accents and softens the rigid lines of the gladiola stems. ✿

Lichen-covered branches combine with spherical yellow Billy buttons to create an abstract arrangement in an unusual, primitive container. This wooden mortar from Indonesia was once used to pound grain, but its proportion and weight are ideal for supporting a tall floral arrangement, and it beautifully complements the tribal textiles and accessories in this home. The wonderfully textured branches, native to the Pacific Northwest, were purchased at a local flower shop, and the Billy buttons came from a craft store that stocked dried floral supplies. Once I decided to use the mortar, I wedged a block of floral foam inside to secure the branches and stems. One at a time, I inserted two or three branches into the mortar, anchoring them in the floral foam base, followed by the Billy buttons. Because of their comparatively thin stems, from across the room the Billy buttons appear to float without any support. The placement of this arrangement draws the eye to the boldly patterned panel of African fabric on the wall behind it, and the arrangement is visually counterbalanced by the squat vessel to its right. ✿

A floral arrangement is beautiful all by itself, but when deciding where to place yours, consider integrating it as part of a composition of elements on a surface, rather than having it stand starkly alone. It should complement and harmonize with the accessories surrounding it.

Poppies are a delicate, almost ethereal flower, with thin petals and a beautiful form. A poppy's gossamer quality allows light to shine through it in a way that makes the flower appear translucent. Here, red and orange Icelandic silk poppies are arranged in an orange glass vase with an elliptical shape. Some low stems form a sort of collar around the mouth of the container, while a few taller ones give the arrangement its height and its loose, airy quality. ✿

All-white arrangements look very fresh, and this grouping of white silk flowers on an entry table is quite convincing. In this photograph, a new galvanized flower bucket contains eighteen stems—six each of lilac, zinnia, and delphinium. I began the arrangement with the tallest stems—the delphiniums, then added lilacs to soften the look, filling in with the zinnias. The result is a lush arrangement with a commanding presence that was relatively inexpensive to create and that works beautifully next to a fragment of garden statuary and a round metal finial. ✿

Stunning in late afternoon sunlight, this loose and informal arrangement of faux garden flowers in a tall ceramic cylinder is dominated by yellow, white, and blue Dutch irises. This beautiful spring statement seems perfectly proportioned for a living room sofa table. The abundance of stems, placed one at a time, holds everything together, with no floral foam required to anchor the arrangement. When building a self-supporting arrangement, you begin by placing a single stem in a container. Generally speaking, I start by building a foundation with greens, adding blossoms last. In an open-mouthed vessel such as this, that first stem will naturally lean against the rim, at something close to a forty-five degree angle. The second stem should be placed in opposition to the first, so that the stems create a standing X inside the container. If this first pair of stems is located at, say, twelve and six o'clock, place the second pair at three and nine o'clock. Work consecutive stems into the available spaces, and you'll quickly find you've created a thicket of crossed stems and leaves that will now hold additional stems exactly where you insert them, in this case allowing the iris to stand vertically. You won't achieve this effect by jamming a bunch of flowers in a vase; stems really must be placed individually or they'll appear crowded, without the subtle interplay between them you see here. Since the faux stems you purchase will be a uniform length, it's a good idea to use your wire cutters to vary the lengths by an inch or two, which will result in an arrangement with a more pleasing and natural appearance. ✿

If you've ever spent an evening shifting in your seat or craning your neck in an attempt to carry on a conversation with a dinner companion opposite you, you know how disconcerting a tall flower arrangement on a dining table can be. Keep these centerpieces low enough for your guests to see one another, and consider adding height with tall taper candles instead.

A classic Chinese celadon vase is the foundation for this dynamic, asymmetrical arrangement. Protea flowers, flocked in cool gray tones, contrast with large, exotic leaves that provide the assemblage with its tension and counterbalance. The muted colors of the stems and the sweeping, natural gestures of the palm frond contribute to this arrangement's sophisticated appeal. ✿

Dried hydrangea heads nestled in a foundation of faux camellia greens are the dominant feature of this autumn harvest arrangement in an old tin bucket. A mix of dried and silk stems blend to create a rich design statement that also includes graceful extensions of faux pokeberry, wormwood, wheat, and bear grass, all of which contribute height to the arrangement.

Because dried hydrangea heads are large and somewhat fragile, you don't find them as frequently as you do other varieties of dried flowers. In late summer and early fall, however, fresh hydrangea appears briefly and in abundance at both city markets and rural farm stands. They'll dry beautifully and will hold their color for a long time—a year or more—under the right conditions. The best way to dry them is to hang them upside down, out of direct sunlight, in a spot with good air circulation (an attic, toolshed, or closet work nicely). Hanging them prevents the weight of the head from bending the stem as it dries, which would result in a droopy appearance. You can dry hydrangeas individually, or simply bind a bunch of stems with a rubber band or piece of wire and suspend them over a nail or a coat hanger.

In constructing most arrangements, I often begin by establishing a foundation of greens, then add the dominant blossoms. In this case I used the hydrangea heads first to establish an expansive visual statement, securing the stems in a block of floral foam wedged at the bottom of the bucket. Next, I filled in around the hydrangea heads with all the other elements mentioned above.

When creating an arrangement of this scale, once you've established its basic form, stand back from time to time as you work and assess where it's going, adding stems as needed. Will the arrangement be seen from all sides? It isn't necessary to place materials on the side of an arrangement that will face a wall. Try to minimize handling dried hydrangea heads, since they shatter easily.

A larger container is appropriate for this type of arrangement, and the bucket I used gives this floral presentation a rustic feel. You could achieve a more contemporary look by using a cylinder vase, a cube, or any other wide-mouthed vessel that appeals to you. ✿

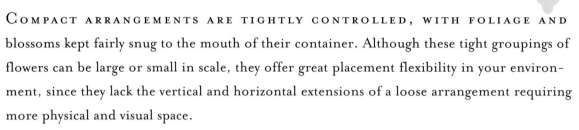

COMPACT DESIGNS

COMPACT ARRANGEMENTS ARE TIGHTLY CONTROLLED, WITH FOLIAGE AND blossoms kept fairly snug to the mouth of their container. Although these tight groupings of flowers can be large or small in scale, they offer great placement flexibility in your environment, since they lack the vertical and horizontal extensions of a loose arrangement requiring more physical and visual space.

You can use any flowers in a compact arrangement, but most will need their stems cut fairly short. In many cases, these arrangements are constructed by securing stems in a block of floral foam that's been wedged inside a low container.

When cutting stems short or stripping leaves, save the extras in a small box. Use that mixed supply of leaves and stems to add textural interest in other arrangements, like the tumbler on page 98. Another example is the arrangement of carnations opposite, which features a very different type of leaf as a collar.

These compact faux floral arrangements are ideal for a desk, dining table, nightstand, or any other surface whose function dictates your ability to reach or see around and beyond the flowers. They add grace and color to a surface, without impeding its use.

The freshness, purity, and elegance of this compact white and green arrangement in a silver tumbler make it an ideal centerpiece for a seasonal holiday or even a wedding. Simply assembled in a small block of floral foam, this composition began with magnolia leaf, followed in order by viburnum, paperwhite, dusty miller, stephanotis, and maidenhair fern. Imagine how this arrangement would shimmer on a table scattered with white votive candles and glassware. ✿

This lush arrangement, which makes a striking addition to a Thanksgiving table, suggests the abundant bounty of autumn, yet it's small in scale. The stems inside the glass cylinder are concealed by tiny ears of Indian corn. The rich purple of the anemones contrasts with the gold sunflowers, while hops, kangaroo paws, bittersweets, and pyracantha berries provide textural counterpoints and visual interest. ❀

This tightly packed grouping of black-eyed Susans in a terra-cotta pot is about contrasts in scale. Small bunches of flowers secured in floral foam were augmented by some larger individual blossoms. Combining the two sizes creates a sort of visual rhythm as your eye moves around the arrangement. ✿

A clay crock of ruffled sunflowers by an open door seems simultaneously to absorb and transmit a golden light. The low-fired, wide-mouthed olive jar is a classic shape that nicely supports the visual weight of the flowers and greens contained within. Five faux sunflowers have been placed inside the crock and positioned face forward for maximum impact. No floral foam was necessary to anchor the stems, because the stiff leaves of the greens lock the stems in place. ✿

Fresh carnations are available all year long, and no matter when you display them, they never seem out of season. This compact silk arrangement of pale pink, hot pink, and red carnations is anchored in a block of floral foam inside a crackle glazed ceramic flowerpot. A collar of hydrangea greens left over from another arrangement adds definition, and the dome shape created by the tightly packed blossoms contrasts attractively with the cone shape of the container. ✿

Six short stems of pink dahlias make an abundant display in a ceramic crock, creating a compact arrangement with a summer feeling that looks at home almost anywhere. ✿

This tight arrangement of fully blown orange parrot tulips in an hourglass-shaped ceramic vessel is as vibrant as flames and adds a dramatic splash of color to a home office. ✿

All flowers are beautiful in sunlight, but remember that both silk and dried florals, like any textile, will begin to fade with constant exposure to ultraviolet light.

This compact grouping of ranunculus in a ceramic cachepot is a perfect arrangement for a bedside, side table, or other small space. The floral components are neatly contained, and it adds a punch of color and texture that's both graphic and clean. Three delicately tinted shades of silk ranunculus blossoms were used here, with coleus leaves augmenting the stems' "natural" foliage and adding a hint of a deeper color.

Like so many arrangements in this book, I began this one by matching a container to the flowers, then wedging a block of floral foam inside it. I trimmed some of the ranunculus stems to different lengths so that the finished arrangement would have a natural appearance. I inserted stems into the foam until the arrangement felt sufficiently abundant, then tucked some coleus leaves in between the flowers. I had also used wire cutters to remove the buds from most of the stems, enabling me to place a few buds where I chose to, rather than have the "blossom, smaller blossom, bud" configuration of the stem repeat itself in a predictable, unnatural pattern. Like fresh flowers, faux flowers can be manipulated to suit your design requirements. Is the stem too long? Cut it. Too many leaves on a stem? Remove them. Don't feel bound to use a stem the way in which it was manufactured. That would be very limiting, and in many cases, would result in a far less interesting arrangement. ✿

A bright, dome-shaped arrangement of zinnias, dahlias, and black-eyed Susans is softened by a few stems of Queen Anne's lace. Their colors are strongly contrasted against a dark turned wooden bowl in an environment decorated with midcentury modern furnishings.

This arrangement began as a pile of hot colored stems next to a wooden bowl. After I secured a block of floral foam inside the container, I began to establish the arrangement's dome shape, starting with the top. I inserted a stem dead center, determining the arrangement's height, then spaced four or five additional flowers around the perimeter. Working within the boundaries set by just this handful of stems, I used the rest of the flowers to fill in the voids, building a lush, tight cluster, finally adding the Queen Anne's lace as a textural accent. Notice the way the blossoms overlap and the way some of them are slightly turned. These were deliberate design choices and are partly what gives this arrangement its softness and grace. ✿

The cool blue, purple, and pink colors of this arrangement come from an assortment of silk hydrangeas, anemones, tulips, and freesias, tightly packed into a contemporary aluminum vase. Without any floral foam in the vase, I began to arrange the large hydrangea heads, quickly establishing the arrangement's basic form and creating a thicket of stems that would support the stems to follow. I then added the tulips and anemones, finally inserting some freesia, with its very different and extended form.

One of the things I find interesting about this arrangement is the way the tulips appear—some tight in bud, others fully blown, as if the heat of the house has forced them to open up, despite their tight quarters nestled in among the hydrangeas. I manipulated the tulip petals to make it looks as if they had been picked at different times, and they also appear to be at different points in their life cycle. Additionally, I'd removed some of the florets from the hydrangea's head to create some spaces for those tulips. Don't hesitate to use your clippers to make a faux flower work for you. ❁

A summer dining table is graced by a white ruffled bowl of rose blossoms placed atop two cake stands ringed by seashells, creating an unusual tower configuration. The interesting thing about this arrangement is the way the bowl of rose blossoms relates to the ripples of the pottery and the pearly quality of the shells. The bowl can easily be moved to another location after lunch, perhaps to a bedside table. ✿

This sophisticated and richly textured little arrangement is one of my favorites. It combines silk and dried materials in a way that really fools the eye. There's something about introducing seedpods, pinecones, or other natural elements in a faux arrangement that, for me, really elevates it to another level. The components I've used in this piece would adapt beautifully to a wreath design that would be appropriate for any season, and, like this arrangement, would work nicely almost anywhere. The container, an inexpensive small metal bucket with a wire handle and rust-colored patina, was purchased new at a garden center.

After wedging a square of floral foam inside the bucket, I began constructing the arrangement by inserting short stems of faux coleus greens to create a collar around the rim of the container, followed by a half-dozen dried poppy seedpods. I then added five or six yellow silk tea roses, followed by a few sprigs of dusty miller for contrast, and some tiny pinecones I purchased, already attached to wooden floral picks. The arrangement makes an attractive centerpiece for a table and could easily be reproduced in multiples to dress several tables for a party or special event. ✿

WHILE FLORAL ARRANGEMENTS ARE CREATED BY THE HUMAN HAND AND eye, a planting—or an imitation of the real thing—reflects nature's creation, and the relationships between leaves and blossoms are predetermined. If you've managed to kill every African violet your sister's ever given you, a faux or permanent plant is an ideal alternative, bringing color, grace, and a sense of life to any environment.

Many charming and convincing permanent plants are available in the marketplace today, offering most of the same pleasures you'd derive from having live plants in your home. Since water, light, and temperature considerations aren't part of the equation, faux plants can be enjoyed in places it would be impractical to put a live plant, such as inside a bookcase or in a windowless room.

Most faux plants have a thick single stem, which can be anchored in floral foam inside its container. The foam can be concealed by moss, stones, or another attractive medium, and you can choose from a wide range of containers—clever little cachepots, softly glazed ceramic containers, even your standard clay flower pot. Best of all, you'll never have to ask a neighbor to water these plants while you're away.

A bathroom is brightened by a single wild daffodil in a glazed ceramic cylinder. The stem and straplike foliage are gently bowed, giving this arrangement a very natural appearance. A bit of moss conceals the block of floral foam used to anchor the stem. ✿

Here, a white dendrobium orchid adds a light touch and point of contrast in a dark decorating scheme, and employs another natural-looking material—faux Spanish moss—to conceal the floral foam at its base. ✿

Moss is a very useful and versatile component for floral designers, whether they're working with faux or live plant material. An element often seen in high-end floral designs, moss can help make a sophisticated planting just a bit more special. Used with live plants, moss helps prevent the soil from drying out too quickly. For our purposes, moss is used to conceal the "works"—the floral foam used to anchor a faux plant's stem—and to add an attractive natural component to the presentation.

You'll find three basic types of moss sold in florists, nurseries, and national chain craft stores. The one shown here is a faux version of Spanish moss, an air plant associated with Southern waterways and antebellum estates that is often seen swaying gracefully from cypress and live oak trees. For the floral industry, Spanish moss is sterilized and packaged in plastic bags. Another type, sheet moss—sometimes labeled "decorator moss"—grows in spreading patches with shallow root systems that can be literally peeled from the forest floor (examples can be seen on page 118 and 124). A third type, called reindeer moss, grows in rounded clumps and is used in things like topiary craft projects involving hot glue.

Spanish moss remains supple and easy to work with, even after it has dried out. Sheet moss, however, becomes a bit stiff as it dries, though a light misting with a spray bottle will refresh it, making it pliable again. Keep in mind that direct sunlight will cause moss to fade and brown over time. Luckily, it's inexpensive and easily replaced.

Like me, you may sometimes have an opportunity to gather your own moss. A word of caution: Before you use freshly harvested moss indoors, put it in a plastic bag in the freezer for a day or two to prevent introducing unwanted critters into your home. ✿

A shallow rectangular Chinese planter is a traditional foundation for a fresh-looking group of faux spring paperwhites. These stems are as convincing as the real thing and are authentic in their detailing, down to their exposed bulbs. A block of floral foam is all that was required to provide a base in which to anchor the paperwhites' heavy-gauge wire stems, secured simply by being pushed directly into the foam. I spaced the bulbs with enough "breathing room" that the blossoms above wouldn't appear too crowded, and the resulting effect is natural and unforced. A layer of sheet moss—sometimes sold as "decorator moss"—conceals the floral foam in which the wire stems are secured. A layer of pebbles would be an appropriate alternative. ✿

Faux blooming hyacinth bulbs, convincing down to the last detail, are displayed in traditional jewel-toned glass forcing vases, which reveal their root systems. The only thing missing is the fragrance. ✿

A simple terra-cotta rose pot is an ideal container for this "planting" of pale tea roses, a small floral statement that's a perfect decorative accent in any environment and one that couldn't have been simpler to assemble. This tiny rose bush has a thick single stem in which all the individual flower stems are bound. I wedged a small square of floral foam inside the rose pot, then spent a few moments opening up and manipulating the bush's stiff, straight wires. I turned the rose heads this way and that, giving the plant some natural gestures, then simply pushed the stem securely into the foam. The result is an arrangement of understated beauty that would be at home on a windowsill, nightstand, or dining table. It would also make a perfect gift. ✿

An old violet stand discovered in a dark corner of an antique shop is back in service, holding a variety of beautiful clay flowerpots glazed in soft neutral colors. Unlike their delicate natural counterparts, these faux African violets will withstand direct light and temperature fluctuations. Remember, however, that both silk and dried florals will begin to fade with constant exposure to ultraviolet light. ❁

This three-ball wire topiary form, still threaded with dead vines, was rescued from the garage and given a new life. The wire form was anchored in floral foam wedged in a clay flowerpot, then dressed out with a bit of moss around its base. In just a few minutes—and at very little expense—the topiary form was worked with a few lengths of faux ivy. I simply tucked the end of a length of ivy to the form, then wrapped it around the sphere, occasionally threading the vine through the form to secure it. The old vine was left in place to add depth and character, and the result is an ivy topiary that appears alive and well. Where this topiary certainly has great versatility in terms of its placement in a home, it would also be ideal in an office environment. ✿

Two wire topiary forms, purchased at a national chain garden center, form the basis of these plantings. Honeysuckle vine in a clay pot washed with acrylic paint is "trained" on a wire ring, and a length of ivy is wound around a spiral, illustrating two very quick and easy faux floral projects. Both forms are then secured in a block of floral foam wedged inside the pots and concealed with a bit of moss. ❀

An orchid is another plant available year-round, and a faux orchid is a very convincing approximation of the real thing. The wire stem has been given a natural contour, and the plant's visible roots are contrasted against polished black stones. Anchored in floral foam wedged inside a square ceramic container, this pink vanda plant graces a kitchen counter, where it can be enjoyed throughout the day. ✿

A cluster of faux succulent houseplants in small ceramic containers adds life and a tropical texture to a sunny kitchen window.

These delightful little plants were purchased just as you see them, with thick central stems that were secured in floral foam wedged inside their containers. Care was taken to match the plants to appropriate, complementary containers, because on this diminutive scale, the vessel is an integral part of the design statement. Polished black stones conceal the foam in which the stems are anchored, and the only care these plants require is a periodic rinsing and air drying to remove dust. ✿

A small galvanized pail contains a whimsical faux cherry tomato plant. Staked with green bamboo, it's authentic in its detailing, down to tiny yellow blossoms along its laterals. It would brighten a deck, patio, fire escape, or kitchen, and it never fails to convince—then amuse—guests invited to sample the ripe fruits. This is pure fun. ❀

Credits

✿ TUCKER ROBBINS
33-02 Skillman Avenue
Long Island City, NY 11101
(212) 366-4427
www.tuckerrobbins.com
  wooden candle holder, *50, 51*
  Spider's Nest Table, *48*
  wooden morter, *85*
  birch twig table, *106*

✿ POTLUCK STUDIOS
23 Main Street
Accord, NY 12404
(845) 626-2300
Fax: (845) 626-2321
www.potluckstudios.com
  flower pot, *6*
  platter, *43*
  cachepot, *19*
  flower pot, *21*
  vases, *45*
  bowl, *46*
  flower pot, *89*
  cylinder vase, *90*
  cachepot, bowl, and bedding, *106*
  ruffled cakestands and bowl, *112*
  cylinder planter, *115*
  flowerpots, *122-123, 127*

✿ GREEN COTTAGE
1204 State Road 213
High Falls, NY 12440
(845) 687-4810
  woven strap totebag, *22*
  floral frogs, *21*
  footed bowl, *93*

✿ FRANK SWIM ANTIQUES
430 Warren Street
Hudson, NY 12534
(518) 822-0411
Blenko vases, *19, 24, 28, 66, 67, 83, 86, 87*

✿ CLAUDIO STALLING
WOODTURNING
(845) 626-5530
www.turningartstudio.com
turningart@hvi.net
  Turned bowls, *31, 58, 70, 71*

✿ POTTERY BARN
  Square silver tray, *98, 47*
  Woven square tray, *48, 31*
  Glass cylinder vase, *41*
  Vase and potpourri, *59*
  Lantern and candle, *61*
  Woven round tray, *70*
  Glass vase, *80*
  Vase, *110*

✿ PIER 1 IMPORTS
  Wooden bowl, *31 (upper right)*, *109*
  Table, *19*
  Woven chair, *20*
  Table lamp, *106*

Resources

✿ Aria
San Francisco, CA
415-433-0219
Antique garden and architectural
ornaments, lighting, and furniture.

✿ Anthropologie
Stores nationwide.
800-309-2500
www.anthropologie.com
Tabletop, home accessories.

✿ Australian Fabric
Wholesalers Pty. Ltd.
Abbotsford, Australia
(03) 9417-4333
Floral tapestries, chintzes, and silks
from around the world.

✿ Botanica
San Diego, CA
619-294-3100
Stylish floral design, smart, chic
accessories.

✿ Britex Fabrics
San Francisco, CA
415-392-2910
www.britexfabrics.com
Large selection of fabrics from
around the world.

✿ Chelsea Garden Center
New York, NY
212-929-2477
Indoor and outdoor evergreens,
trees, containers.

✿ Chintz & Co.
Victoria, British Columbia
250-388-0996
Floral fabrics and accessories.

✿ Cost Plus
Stores worldwide.
800-777-3032
www.costplus.com
Home furnishings and accessories
from around the world.

✿ Crate & Barrel
Stores nationwide and catalog.
800-967-6696
www.crateandbarrel.com
Home furnishings and accessories.

✿ Designer Fabric Outlet
Toronto, Ontario
416-531-2810
Wide selection of designer fabrics.

✿ Fidalgo's
British Columbia
Coquitlam Store 604-944-9438
Maple Ridge Store 604-460-9119
White Rock Store 604-531-8733
Silk flowers, dried flowers, containers
and vases.

✿ Garden Home
Berkeley, CA
510-599-7050
Interior furniture, topiary, orchids,
accessories inspired by the garden.

✿ The Garden Trellis
New Orleans, LA
504-861-1953
Garden ornaments old and new,
plants and flowers.

✿ The Gardener
Berkeley, CA
510-548-4545
Fine merchandise inspired by the
garden, from rugs to vases.

✿ Ikea
Stores nationwide and catalog.
800-959-3349
www.ikea.com
Contemporary home furnishings,
vases, and accessories.

✿ Jo-Ann Fabrics and Crafts
Stores nationwide.
877-465-6266
www.joann.com
Fabrics, ribbons, and trimmings.

✿ Lowe's Home Centers
Stores nationwide.
1-800-44LOWES
www.lowes.com
Containers, housewares, and
furnishings.

✿ Michael's Crafts
Stores nationwide.
800-MICHAELS
www.michaels.com
Silk and dried flowers, arranging
tools and accessories, ribbons and
finishings.

✿ Pier 1 Imports
Stores nationwide.
800-245-4595
www.pierone.com
Colorful imported vases, planters, etc.

✿ Pottery Barn
Stores nationwide and catalog.
800-922-5507
www.potterybarn.com
Silk and dried flowers, attractive, affordable vases, and accessories.

✿ Restoration Hardware
Stores nationwide and catalog.
800-762-1005
www.restorationhardware.com
Vases, silk and dried flowers, and garden-inspired accessories.

✿ Silk Botanica
South San Francisco, CA
888-889-8638
customerservice@silkbotanica.net
Silk and dried flowers, containers and vases.

✿ Smith & Hawken
Stores nationwide and catalog.
800-776-3336
www.smithandhawken.com
Garden accessories, vases, etc.

✿ Target
Stores nationwide.
888-304-4000
www.target.com
Affordable, decorative home furnishings and flower supplies.

Acknowledgments

Anyone who's been involved in the production of a book knows that it takes the collective talents and efforts of many people to bring something beautiful to life. We extend sincere thanks to our good friend Emma Sweeney at Harold Ober Associates, who, by happy coincidence, is also our literary agent. We're also grateful to Roy Gumpel for his photographic talents and the strong visual sensitivity he brings to the images throughout this book.

Big thanks are due to the kind and talented folks at Chronicle Books, including Azi Rad for her help in developing the book's aesthetic focus, Gretchen Scoble for creating its beautiful design, Jodi Davis for her attention to the important details, and especially our editor Mikyla Bruder, both for her clear insights and her continued encouragement throughout the entire creative process.

We're particularly grateful to Nancy Tong at Silk Botanica, who so generously supplied all the extraordinary silk floral material used throughout the book. The variety and craftsmanship in this floral line is unparalleled.

For loaning us many of the furnishings and accessories used to create the images in this book, we extend our gratitude to Christiane Dwyer at Pier 1 Imports and to Leigh Oshirak at Pottery Barn. We're especially thankful to Tucker Robbins for allowing us access to his New York City showroom of extraordinary tribal furniture and artifacts, and to Frank Swim of Hudson, New York, for letting us borrow from his spectacular inventory of Blenko Glass. Special thanks to Karen Skelton and Richard Siegel of PotLuck Studios in Accord, New York, who provided us with their beautiful contemporary ceramics. Thanks also to Marie Wintriss for coming up with the idea.

For allowing us to photograph in their homes, we also thank David Urso and Dennis Nutley, Emma Sweeney, Karen Skelton and Richard Siegel, Steve Gorn and Barbara Bash, Charles and Hilton Purvis, and Gregory and Arlene Chiaramonte.

For your generosity, your cooperation, and your friendship, we thank you all.